A HELLSMOUTH F0R ORPHEUS

Books by David Appelbaum

First Stop
On Count
The Sawn Bench
An Alchemist at Heart
The Earthworm Jar
The Book of Nine Elixirs
The Shock of Love

A Hellsmouth
for Orpheus

David Appelbaum

CODHILL PRESS
New Paltz . New York

Library of Congress Cataloging-in-Publication Data

Appelbaum, David
   A Hellsmouth for Orpheus
   David Appelbaum
      p. cm.
   ISBN 1-930337-11-6 (alk. paper)
   I. Poetry. 2. David Appelbaum- I. Title
   PS3551.P557H45 2003
   811'.54—dc21

CONTENTS

"In my opinion the didactic art is an ancient one, but those among the old writers who practiced it were afraid of the odium of the name and so took refuge in a disguise. For this purpose some, like Homer, Hesiod and Simonides, used poetry, others, religious rites and prophecies, I mean the school of Orpheus and Musaios."

Plato, *Protagoras* 316 d

BONE STRAW

[1]

There is a grace before
    all things

        Suppose so

Then you are right to

    make sacrifice

        onion grass
        on a mortar shell casing
        of your father

        on an oak stand
            bought in Ithaca:

            come astride me now

    let the vocative
        be

        April light
            blazed
            before all things

            your one eye
                Mister Horus

        If you come
        it is time

[2]

Don't tell time

   Wait a little
   in dervish dress
      broad rim
      motionless

   in air

   hem
   of a robe
   opens

          an altar
          to mundane forms
          life below

             Didn't I call
             for sacrifices'

             ultimate cost?

          You've come so late,
          butterfly,

             why do you wake me
             digressing in
             long winters'
             love betrayed
             passing
                northward

          You speak
             my tongue

[3]

Go, leave

my pen is afire with
encaustic
      ciphers
      on cave limestone

            drooling around the edges

            would you say eros
            is so?

These caves
millennia past

            roused
            burning pitch
            in a black rock bowl

            twin wisps of
            incense
            savagely
            to the low ceiling

in Persephone's
dream
one night before being
            raped

Go, do not turn your back

[4]

You think
     if a man
          thinks of me

          any more than you,

          I will return with

          gods of fire—
                    Hephaestus, Thoth
                    Zagreus
                    soi-meme

          you think
                    I am being rash
                    carelessly
                    blinding myself

Then erect my ruins
     by the well

          Offer up a prayer with
          the sweetest
          herbs

                    I am ready

                    to meet,
                    dear
                    Godly one

[5]

phenomenality

    begun as idealism would
    rather ante up

        Dionysos as anti-
        God

        life-foreshortened
        brilliance
        procures
        solace, Zarathustra

Here, picayune heart,
    scroll
    down like a birdnest

    their reality,

        a fulcrum to
        transcend
        impossibility

    you drive me
    deep
    into your words

    where my seed will
    fecundate

[6]

Secret

must

on the sofa's

     twin arms
     are her snakes' fangs—
     Medusa—

     bent posterior
     offers

       a hermetic

       look
       before
       asking

       what you taste of,
          proofed

What is error
if not this
mad dash
to put down
     a bed of ashes

     egregious as sin

[7]

I don't like secret
    bliss any more

        I'm old, poorer
        than Baucis

            bow kiss

        your tears,
        short of the altar,

        lave your feet
        in silence

            you've just gone

        when punishment
        is obvious
            truth

            imprisoned in a cave
            of a jealous
            dragon

Honor the secret
    flaw of the poem,
        bow kiss

[8]

No one is entitled to sin

   against the word

      In that
      I've forgotten
      oracle prayers

        Just listen

            for the separation

            Let me home
            Circe

            unnerve me from your spell

            cast me
            here

    ashtray black
    burnt pitch

      August's dog is
      when they finally
      kill the bear
      of this silent cave

[9]

Aromatic
      salt, sniff

            February mist
            yesterday, today
            a butterfly

Is today's

            salt more than I can bear

            aging
            gravel
            in the voice?

Do not grant me secrets
I have not earned

            Need I say

            salt is
            unshackling
            the tongue's

                  heavy
                  metallic lies

Envy sings with its violent beauty
            whether you like it
            there or not

[10]

You have an end
    somewhere there

        at the beginning of the prayer
        when you burn
        the paper mask

            throw its ash
            at the goose

                forgive the brilliance,
                it is not theirs
                but the fire's

        three hundred
        prostrations
        for the name
        they sing, *hamsa*

            I do not want you
            back
            without scars
                where you've burned

            Go, I am hard

        rosemary for your hair
        cinnabar too
        obvious
        at last

            you who
            lurk in the bark
            looking

[11]

Did you turn the page
    in hope
    of a reprieve

        from immortal misery

        exposed as you
        now to the eye
        who reads
        along

        unknowingly bound

        to ivy, to stone

        in a work against a betrayal
        of all beauty:

            this grace
            watches
            our every move

                eye searches
                soul
                for affirmation

                love comes like that

                    after hours

QUARTET IN TWO-TIME

[1]

Jangled,
still
   stiff to

  want to faun
  away the afternoon

        it's goats
            the day you

           absolve me from

           pain
       deceit—
              give it a whirl,

    seek
       the obvious

           jangling unsubtitled
             in the wings

                 of an easy chair
                 on the outerbridge
                 crossing
                 of cacophony:

Pull chalk on it and see.

[2]

Is somewhere in the heart

   calling for

regurgitation,

      voice *primitif*

         swallowed shortly after birth —
never more
   than this, saying

   love

  saying says when says says
   anything at all

    if you find it sufficient.

      What's lost memory:

       take skin

          stretched for guile
          sunlight dreams

          irresponsible as flesh

          tender as the moment

            coming
            comes

[3]

Lover each night new
	you, Aphrodite, from Thebes or
		Thrace

	bootlegger rum

Gee, will you survive

	bivouacs to put on
	their whirligig side

		Write me letters
			that imply
			sincerity
				or without shame

		the earnest opposite
			to my Orphic reverie

			that wants to
			become song

				On the morrow
				love again comes

					in the hallow of
					an orange-winged
					moth
					spearing the flame

[4]

Not as concrete as perfume
only the fifth room

    will have a quintessence that
    rises to the nostrils

        like fire

            Yesterday I burned

           pine pitch
                  on the altar at Ephesos,
                  Saint John

                      you were lavender-bathed

                      no belly for a blonde
                      triadic

[5]

Transport a body
    to hang in a tree

            like a vampire tale
                        truth is
            becoming

                    loose gossip again

                    justified verve
                    no verbiage but
                    rounded corners

                    so no prayer can use it

                    to master himself

                            no other master either,
        but each
            is own,
                    master to each —

                        as masters taught —

                            light as it is
                            is it light as

                            it again is?

                                It is lighter this time
                                than it ever before or
                                since

17

[6]

Late but you
     bothered to come, late,

          unwanted, unransomed
          In ways before
                    you reform who
                    I can love,
                    you must have
                              patience
                              more stubborn than art.

     It was evening one spring
       crouching

          by erasure that you
                    smudged

     indecision

          inadvertently
                    intentional

                         as geese singled out stars
                         to shimmer as globes
                         of the universe that
                         grunts and groans

          you sent them
                    longing
                    for the way home

[7]

Do not be jealous

of endings,

> they aren't
> to say life stops here

>> Trade these forceps
>> meant for premature birth

> Fire your personal trainer,

>> sincerity is on the rise

>>> Let go

>> It all will return
>> *in res*

> No serious leak,
> cottonball,

>> just juxtapose
>> the noun with the tongue

>> linger

>> grow flexible

>>> like stone
>>> like crocus under stone
>>> like crocus
>>> unfurls

[8]

Bark
        daily,

                your reverence,

                love me,
                I desire the words

                themselves

                        in joint repetition

                        as mirrors seize
                        the likes of me

Quiet, jet, say

        Love is

                carefree as a spasm
                seven miles long

Stand at the gate
and bark,
Orpheus,

no one to
bark at
but the dead

[9]

Does a run
     end
          where your tongue
                    bends straining

               to music

               of sinew

               tight over bone

          as the pan tilts
                         with a feather

                    toward everything said
                    adequately
                    with much saliva?

     [10]

Squirt

     the word
     eo ipso
     into real

          incense

from Phoenicia
on the altar

Don't put
rosewater
on the needle

Regard whose subject
pants for

on silver wings,

    an angel

        may call my name,

           Orpheus

[11]

No man withholds

  fate

    or relishes
making amends

    even well-met
by those decrees

But I will not disturb

    the speech of others

        if only you speak to me,

        wood against
        thick skin—

            no other
            still waits
            to meet you

                as I do

[12]

Ivy

    is over
        before ever finishing

    love

        is a rush after
        the muslin-covered

        clay pot brought
        in hope

        only yesterday home

You end, a cunning

trail up the side of the

house
Search there
if you're agile
beguiled by

a thirst
up your vein

INSURRECTION SULTANA

[1]

I can hear highway glow

    a new one
leading
    nowhere new

    In Thrace, the sun is
      a pyramid

               you can see
               everything

I saw you yesterday

    a match lifting
frankincense

      you lay open
      lips
      upon lips

              Cease memory,

         no longer

             can I hear cars
             rustling

                    hair damp
                    dropping to the
                    floor

[2]

I will not lie with you

    with another
    in you

        as one reaches for a feather

I am that cruel
    even more provoking

    Love is our test

        we survivors
        learn by failing

The senses dictate
    what said why

        That is appetite
        seen as such

            self-control prevents
            no denial

                where negation is

You are a negative

    I lie

[3]

Late light before rain

      nature is observed
      when eros
           disturbs the breath

in heights

         with questions
             in the mirror

         You love who
         you can see

            no other, beloved

the more you are
everywhere

    on each woman's face

         Forgive me
         your glory-
             body

            I desire
            you
                  myself

[4]

Forgive me,
      grace long since said
      a blessing

      since you question
      authority

            but you see this
            becoming
                        stunning
                        without
                        looks

                        are you cause
                        or product,

                        ubiquity?

      Did I ever say
      permanence

      features in life?

            Forgive us our daily bread
            for sins
            we never knew

            shoulder wrenched
                  where you sleep
                              while the sun
                              ploughs beneath

[5]

Goat no more
ever the field
owl would seize
ambit for his brain

Once goat
rammed your throat
to lick your lips
mime your hips

        Your mother lives
        her life through
        you
                according to plan

                    in that cruel form
                    love

                        fails
                        to live
                        the wanted life

        we have words
        to remind
                of that

        may they never
        be unheard

[6]

She has a car

   a house
     interests of her own

the freedom of love's
    being able

        many schools teach
        special
        exercises

        in support

   For all brothers
      it is immoral
          to hinder that

        the payment
        for
            my integrity

            held not too securely

        except thinking
        I know
            my own desire

[7]

Secrets you know
    are here

    you want to know one
    I keep
        from you

  Explain why

        The risk of showing
        is delicious

            That I show

                How?

  Can I
  when it is overwhelming?

        You don't confuse intentions
        when you show
            more words

        Lies are a part of it

                know how,
                you spy

                    Horus

[8]

One ear is deaf
    until it listens

    Many years may pass
        whither it goeth

Then it hears the clatter

    to find music
        in its own way

There is no other way
to practice
than with old masters

        they are the school
        of our time

            Listen,
                    be deaf
                    half a life

                    listen once
                    to
                    traffic

                        glory there

[9]

Love teaches
    the stone
    like a graven pool

        all impulse
        fancy, adventure
        intrigue

                blood up

Dust, wind-blown
pollen

        speaks over years
with wonder

        hollowing
        dead mineral
        for life

                Pools of water
                bob
                in the blue sky

Love teaches
    to drink
                there often

                for Orpheus' face
                sometimes
                watches
                from the bottom

[10]

Oil clings
to the couch

      breath
      of you

the senses
of
wanting no more
than to hold

      I am so spent
      tending
            your damp altar
            on hands
            and knees

rubbing for
fragrance

      a question
      remaining

          already
              forgotten
                again

INDECENCY

[1]

35

Ma faiblesse
   lily of the veil

  yellow honey
  under a hot church sun

      I see patches
      on skin of a shank, *ma faiblesse*

      my indulgence
      my excess
      my indigence

          the tip
          of my tongue
          runneth over

I once knew you decently,
        my dearest

  before the scent
     at the mouth
        of the tunnel

[2]

Do not ask directions
    to break a spell

    It's a one-man job
        too risky to follow
        across the beach
        strewn with strawmen
                on the verge of summer vacation

    Yesterday by a tree
    on Eleventh
        you wrote
    under the tree
    under the leaves of the tree
    dappled
    under ivy I stand
    unknown, alone
                something like that

        weight of iron
        pressed the chest
        against a nest

            Whose will can melt
            such will
            as fate?

    I will not go back now
        I no longer know
        the way

            lost
                in heaven

[3]

That rapture held you
        over a deep
                    dark crack

over ground, under

is of first importance

                Language
                can always find
                        its own way

                        with a voice
                        belonging
                        to nature

                        who speaks
                        the selfsame tongue

                        boiling up clouds
                        of salt sweat

                as a storm jets
                white across the soft
                thigh

                        you sleep
                        panting

[4]

off-track leading
     a couch aside
can promote betting
     a dollop astride

of other mollies
     never coddle
move to moxie
     pass the bottle

                    yet vacate the rational
                    enter the realm
                              of pure song

                    archaic
                              tongue of
                              all speech
                              of heart

                              I can be

                    ma faiblesse

                    plait of silver
                    hair
                    down a slender back

                              chill of a piper
                              runs my spine
                              up, stiff

[5]

I would pass the summer
        with you
                getting nothing much
                done
                        for once—
                                Would it be fun?

                A hack's cry

                        might lead to
                        the big lights
                        stage irony
                        diction
                        a bank account. . .

        Don't say no
        just because you're worthless

                Forget your balls

                        the juice is
                        for something

                        more expensive

[6]

not to substitute or
    lose track
            which you do always

            What I have to say
            is hard
            of hearing

                    because of the twists
                    in the business world

            Is witness
            less to nature's
opulent feather

            than starker realities

                    caves
                    with mouths sealed
                    by bombs

                    whose hours
                    are never precious?

    Is this the death-knowing vigil
            of an initiate

                    who does not substitute
                    longing

                    for longing?

[7]

Cast me another spell,
                    witch

run the creak
backward
        career almost is it

but bind me
with a web
of animal intrigue

        I can
        guts it out with

        my own fluid

                when I'm scared
                take me
                deep
                outahere

                hold nothing back
                this once

[8]

Plexus

hide-organ
seek me
          gnat on a finger

don't keep up
with birdsong
for seed, Thoth,

          own the vocative
          Surely someone else
          lives in here
          unless
          I am all alone
          with you

                    Just my luck
                    caught
                    with my zipper
                    down

[9]

Value is different

    It gets added
    in some mystery

        by an organ
        called the heart

            I must first desire
            to become

                    purge first
                    thoughts of purge

                    for longing
                    is different

                    like cold fur
                    down your neck
                    by the radiator

                    it stinks
                    in your hand

    Longing gets added
    with spikes
    & nails

[10]

No mourning nature poems
  in strange elemental voice

      though I relish good myth

underground
is another erotic
intrigue

      virtual transformation

            Suppose you are
            in the midst

                  of unshirking reality
                  declared
                  each fleeting instant

                        by this grace
                        called
                        life

      No mourning
      no death

   no immortal soul

         no burden
         no no

[11]

lost underground
        lost ground
                near an abyss
                        people ask

What can help?

        Be savvy,

                        exposure
                        but be wary

                        good intentions
                        are endangered

                        by waves
of confession

                        drowned in maudlin

        Boot up
        or get booted

                even penuche counts

[12]

Is there strength, *ma faiblesse?*

Remind me.

>   I keep avoiding
>   your eyes
>   my desire

I long most
for your longing

>   I know no love
>   but the black cave's

>   Is this why Orpheus
>   draws song
>   from the rocks
>   as he leaves

>   that veil
>   that shillelagh
>   on moonstone?

[13]

Barely other than

    calamity
            for the sake of
            readying new stuff

            I saw a giraffe
            once sawed
            in two

            stood with a camel
            fresh out of
            the zoo

ain't she a sweet
beauty?

            saw off
            your other face
                      if you haven't

OPENING

[1]

Niggardly to ask you
    re:distance

  who is subject

to many

  It is wet today
  in Thessaly
  as I write

     ferns bow to
     rushes
     before sacrifice
          fleet and silken

     by light of rushes
     you come to me

       aromatic
       ashen, green

  a desert night

  deep starry Sirius

         dog
         find me home

[2]

Have I changed

   Have I grayed in your magic

      dear mirror?
              Your martial trill
                  finds you golden
                 sere, Athena,

      a thigh under mine

Moonrise
at 2:30
on a dark mailbox

in which your letter
unopened

   alters how I sleep

grazing myself
a Sphinx

   I too know the end

[3]

Again you,
     older,

stand straight
          shy
          slimmer

          a miracle in F

          avenue
          beneath ground
          in a subterranean tunnel

                    twin threads
                    of blue light

                         I look
                         wrong,

                         rather than
                         ravish

[4]

speak
no age
      or all

learn
to teach
as Cleopatra

      if not too young
      for an asp

speak
into my left ear
      let it swallow you

I'll believe when

finally young
enough to

[5]

After wet snow clots
   slam
      wet snow into
      wet snow

I opened

another letter
from you

what number

          dispersed
          in Ephesos
          with Artemis?

the bow
is my silver cup
green silk
          all the way from China

I give these for
whatever gold earnings
beneath
you
          May riches come

this, pray,
this sodden offering

          may find
          smoke

                    to heaven

[6]

slave of love
          you

                    exaggerate

when you chain
          me

because
who could?

No one holds me

when I die

a heart of flesh

in a ring of bone

can

I come
the one
who loves

Eurydice?

[7]

fear, an old trope,

limns it

agape

for Lesbos

come, hold me

caress my balls

    it is a cold
    Alexandrian March

        peepers mate,
        deluded

incomplete

with murmured confusion
        that deletes as it goes

[8]

You open
   twilight

I reach in, desire

    I will touch
    until touch
    returns

       wake
       strong
       full
       a bell

run your tongue
down
over me

burst
the door
of dew

     on burlap
     of the alchemists

     stumps of oak
     daily fern
     winterberry
          eye red
          sulfured

[9]

Whereas to take you

     pinecone
     on the altar

       without tying
       votive joy

to the guide,

       light mist
       in the dark

     whereas to see
     not knowing when you see

       Nyx's

ghosts

or marsh vapor

unwrapping

mineral shoals
miles over Ocean

[10]

Did you come late
    or I tarry?

        Doubt refuses
                wine
                for the asking

    I will come back
                a gazelle
                in a wine bar

                though one other
                intercedes
                on behalf of
    succession

                    by oath
                    I cannot break

                    Anublis,
           open my mouth

to be a soul
        again

        feather-weight
        in the pan

                I come back
                astride you
                        inside
                now suck

[1]

OK, the wind is up again

   I must be
   on earth
   to die

     a flock
     of 5000 doves
     near Lesbos

     veered to my left

       mischief, you

     I know the grove
     where
       you bathe

     I will be blind
       choiceless

          before I finish
          the hymn required

     laurel
     white marble

     a golden bough

[2]

sorrow is ill

    even pained

        the gut of truth
        is peyote

            Remember how
            the eagle
            pierced
            the canvas tent

            how the viscera
            spoke then
            of the need to purge

    listen
        hot lemon juice
        ginseng
        beet
        canned sardines
            come to practicality

[3]

God, whom do I
        want to speak with

                down the black maw?
        Do you know?

                They teem
                around
                blood
                like no tomorrow

                        but who
                                I say
                Who

She must be a wise, gentle sacrifice

[4]

late, you have come
    to face

        my sincerity

            Do I surprise you?

How else, so lost
you are
in your mirror

        wrestling
        the angel
        of reflection

missing
the squint
behind you, love

        by the light
        of stars

are you serious
at play?

[5]

mortal ordinary
multiple many

purity proverb

spring comes again
        with patience

principle order
mental mortal

spirit eternal

  Adonai

        the breath
        saying
        nothing

        a soul
        trails up the road
        a vapor

[6]

the hole you dig
   may be your own
        thinking

dirt

   what is it?

        Lint collecting on a plastic
        lens
        after each blink

   getting off
        is not an option

   putting on gloves
        means no fight
   just as the hand
        in skin
   grips
   the shovel

        dig your way to hackles

[7]

do you glimpse
   squat Aphrodite

   makes a career
   out of rug
     her jealous green eyes

   reek

   motives
       behind death

she loves war
   black pitch
   misshapen flank

     mind the snare

     pray wisely
this world of poverty

   needs
   your drone.

[8]

crone-hoofed turtle

    a stead on my void

        intuit that deep
        cave
        shudder down

    pour molten lead
    into thy gaze

        mind the fire-stone
        that outsmarts

        the sharp, fragrant
        shell burst
        of life

[1]

Walking
    sound,
    a truck

        guns up
    before
        the blessed thing

    tracking

        a head in me

        behind the ears

    secret
    sweet
    ever-flow

        rill
            the oaken grove
        as cloud thunder
        fulgurates

        apocalyptically

        an earthen bell

[2]

Try rub the palms
    in aspirant sand

    as your state

    pains a

    moonfilled

    lake
        along our bed

    countlessly

    before we
      return
        a heart
        embedded in
        skin

        one gold
        bird

                    afloat
                    etherwardly

                    iridescent

                    bud
                    of a moon

[3]

What is the lee
    a pillow

        in wind?

Order a sacrifice

            Willow

            the most holy
            afraid
            in that

does it burn any fire?

In law is
breath
    such the law is—

        elusive or not—

    to make pure
                wind soft

            rapid seas
                    avid
                    lability

[4]

wind decrees

we elope
    when?

        to a stone house
        sage coriander

        assuage
            yarrow
            is yellow

                to let pray

                every
                pennyful of

                wilting stone's

                engraved

        with ancient
        wind's
        decrees
                salome

[5]

Do not invoke
     unknown gods
              ignorant
          of drowning
                    They demand
                    adoration

                    Even to name
                    is a prayer

                              know the ear
                              you pray
                              to

                              an unsung god's

[6]

Once a phoenix
    took
        off

    orange
    underblossoms
    defoliant

            Do not feel

    an incoherence
    comes
            of time
    throne against a window
    but of winterberry
    a passage
    of breath
    illiquid

            one high carriage trail

        argued
        over druids'

                zodiacal
                stone

[7]

Now grace is over

   poured down a cone

   rare as Easter
you,
     at odd times
look clockward

     electric
     aspic

an owl outside

a year
    loquacious
    radiant
    Spanish
I dare not say
   your name
       in bed anymore

[8]

Again you acclimate
    oscillate

    straighten
    sly
    shimmer

        in F

    beneath a world
    bled

        by twin threads
        aster blue

            light

a throng,
            of you

            to lavish

[9]

You who
    you
    ask
        of me

        urge
Are you
  a lesson
      of heart?

             Count me in
             Ring me up
             Ask me over
             Sit me down

                I'm here for
                one
                thing

                unless

                there are two

[10]

Reverse a fold
    unfold or enfold

  a crease

    cuff of some god or king

living
    reversal,

        Hermes,

    bind an eye
    unmold
    mere mold

    pin the pin
    to the underside

    Do I sew too well
    for a thief?

    Raise a hand
    you unband

    a grip
    aggrieve

        a vale
        of fears

        clocking stone

[11]

The cup you keep

   acumen in
must be your friend's

   nervous

      spring appetite

         up the drive
         as it races

      occasionally staunch

   dear barely
    prodigal

   ear

   a robin's

not empty exactly

  but single note

   —beaker

[12]

your habit
    apologizes
        for time that

        mercilessly

        has no desire

        for life-drawing

the stone altar
wakes
    Did we sacrifice
    fire

    so one like
    an other
    stirs

            no more metaphor
            will do

            than grace

[1]

Sacred
    sacerdotal a-grin
    poor herald
        annunciate
        piebald

                as sunrise

    listen, the wise

ass
    lies
    bestrewn
        like worms

this groom
    sound sublunary

        augural
        inaugural

        bore a treetrunk

        white slug

        I prefer jugglery
          to an echo

[2]

pilfer onion grass

    only one
       bulb
              rubbed against a nose

    the wrong way

this turn
    tenderly designed

          for a hearing-aid

          hurray for a drum roll

          practice

Pick words

    from someone's
    actuarial chart

          cash the arrangement

          in for interest

          finger
              the fucker

[3]

Aviary
        eisen glass windmills, for instance

        get good at
        quick
        escapes, squint

                they'll be in
                vogue

        especially after fishing

        for cheap barbs,
                honest
                worms' pay—
                        dirt

                        went awry
                        a stroke

        of crap,

                        while birds
                                tall as you

                        uplift
                        some even
                        pitch

[4]

Stir in

      goddamn

            lichen
            holy inhabitant—
            this realm of alms

      poverty
            grooves election

            challenges erection

                  one
                  gold
                  coin

                  under
                        a collar

      like a cold seat
      a cold

      electric shock
      under
      your ear

[5]

Mastic frantic
    for repair
    Orpheus statue,
    the senses,
            impenitent

                    your
evocative
        heirs let
        duplicity

        without a crease

duck under
rhetoric like

        a cellar door
        mystic

[6]

without meaning

        insisted

     egress is
       a big sky

       constellated by
       cement
         painted

         luminescent black
         chord wheat

           slit sideways

           syncopate
      the idea

[7]

The dog is not my yard
The horse is not my guitar
The tiger is not my spider

     Recently pressed

   oil

        has no middle
        whereas oracles'

          conspiracies make for

        unfinished business

like a fern,

  solace

   for
   cosmogenesis

[8]

Gully
     agonize
          yourself

   down to the sea

  Rock
     occultate
         the reed
             to the river

        the word *home*

           is short
              for soul

  Stick
     estuary
       you

       call to mind

       eminent
       dust-crops

          tight corner

             watch
             stopping

             time
             on the hip

[9]

Oak copper pot

    opalesces green

             end over end

    the wildest

    takes on

    an aspirant

        as wild wrests
        calm
            from calamity

            ends up with friend

            back

            in the aforementioned

  envy
        a risk of rust

[10]

    Butterflies form mullein
      milkweed too

    a fling at the bike

    bilious

        in thin

            ransom

            chill heat
            for a cock moon

            Curious though

            to corral

    sunbeams with

    silver rope
    winged into

        spires
        in
        thin
        air

[11]

For a worm

     argument
         nullifies nothing

             no enemy
             ever
             exudes

       calumny

Energy
  in extra clergy

       tight-collared gut
       a grip on

       effervescence

  a farce

       hard to garble

       back down
          the throat like
          spit

[12]

Blue jay

seriously
        augment

                an ardor
                with flags
                        to flagellate

                a person's
                stuttering
                tongue

                with fir needles
                until

it squeaks

clean, quick
agglutinate

[1]

cannot play,
whatza boy?

    I hurt too much from bridge-
    falling in finesses

    in the only game I know

    thought of another
    hurts at my age

    the fire I'd
    jump into

    melts sinew
    till
    secret juices

    avenge
    in bulbous stems

    like dust
    captioned round the crown
    she anoints

[2]

caterpillar crawl
fate
is life that

cataclysm

    shimmers

    a halo of real disturbance

    winnowing
    monoplane
mourning

this whole febrile vale

[3]

a day in the life of

    no-drone
    no-scam

      try tunes
      not specially tight

    justly tempered

under the hat of a young man

    amazed at this
    'light as silk'

banner
unfurling

its own

[4]

say whose god

        corresponds to
        which plant
                or sun

say God said it

        to satisfy
        sprawl

                        indigent
                        when nothing happens
                        for hours

                        for moments
                        breathe
                        heaven in

                        moaning

I place a lily
        on your navel
        one moonless night

[5]

not allowing you,
    relax, let

        eros say no
        holds
        barred against form

        everything melts

        in indecent war

so let
a wet pillow

    wilt petals of a rose

        they, I send
        a message unto

            wise words would lie
            if they told

            where this
            or anything
                    leads

[6]

Is a bird
        the radii of negatives

                that hollow love?
        Can it sing temperately?

                I would burn my beacon
                        or wand

                                if its one song
                                were to hear
                                my asking

                                it to sing

Then I could ask
        quiet

                where I am
                is so quiet
                I can't hear myself
                think

[7]

shorter than apostrophe to haiku

the short breath ages lungs

 orange rinds dry
 in a green garden
 plastic bag

the joys have triumphed
all three
ear is in thrall
to the assonance
 ashes in a dream
 I don't recall

where it bores
in from outside
where there's nothing

annunciating
everything
that aspirates

so the drum respires
to the trumpet
of a vowel

REIGN OF REASON

[1]

Collect clues
    nothing else

        voice changes
        with second
            adolescence

What is there, no God

    only the monad

        strapped to his seat

            to this day
      toying
            to figure it

      in a dated style

      when it's long been
      too late

      to learn anything new?

[2]

nature and language fascinate
        no denial
                to the same
                        identity
let the connector be ghosted

        Never obvious,
                Magister,
                        never the same

        already

        worn thin
        threadbare

        a toe ring

Be spellbound
        wonder who the reader

        is,
                there below threshold

                        already bound
                        to
                        a
                        fixed concept
                        ahead straight

[3]

'That's right, let's talk to ourselves'

    nature of a dark, set
    breathless
    intoxicant

    I don't want
    your private dreams

        only four buttons
        of happiness
        gathered
            on the kitchen table

Already this dismal
    has more to tease

        despair
            in an absent flair

        not for long
        to be longed for

[4]

a preacher of lateral movement

    once said,
        no senile being
        stands still long enough
        for a target—

           does that make him right

           or rather wrong?

           what's wrong
           with this next whatsyamacallit?

           Ask

    then you drift
        along the great river
        totally at the mercy

        of beneficence

           that you know
           is found
           always next to
           fraud

[5]

the strange truth came
    warped in a pool

    after a day of
    cold rain

            You went to see
            a tree
            but saw a face
            surprised
                    so the years go
                    hopping off with seasons
                    until wood dries from
                    sun, freezes in rain

                    and we are familiar
                    with each other
                    around the eyes, Orphee,

                            while around the head
                            an aura
                            ripens

                            hooded
                            herpetonic

[6]

Absinthe the one who knows
    light shimmers

        in eyes not of the master

                in honesty, hieroglyphs
                do not pertain

                but a divestment

                everyday more
                poor

                        than dress clothes
                        in slow motion

[7]

such work as
	rain dropping from oak boughs

	wrung
	adoringly for God
		I miss it when
		I have it

	mouth wide
		fog
				shrieks
				delirious

				whose work must
				end

				off a beat

[8]

local motive
     gets you

          closer, but

               you are too global,

               errant spring, Eurydice,
                    too archaic
                    for words

     Can you be silent

          until you
          come
          at me
               big breasts
               flapping

                    can you chant

                    flat out

                    penquined
                    on the floor?

DORA RAGES

[1]

fiddle faddle
    riddance

        a *danse reticente*

    why not you?
        Worry not

   it's *a capello*

      hoof

now taught
    on the left runway

      plumage
      cleavage

          bird paste
          on a wig

          scene of
          self-
          chastisement

    outcome
    encore
    dream or deem?

[2]

I would cease

  pitiful
    as a nose ring

  impatient
  dyspeptic

  killer kitsch
  after hours hero

  gimme a morsel
  I wanna broad

      [3]

      secretly tell
          the cook

        I want you
        to open

            me

                bury
                the silver nib

            sly like a lock
            you wound

your utter tongue

a secret lozenge

tasty
wiles sleek

[4]

moral of the Turkish scene:

   diffuse
       costumes
  your eyes
        think back to the bone

        frequently interrupted
        dollop of syrup

  nude cake on
  dry

  velvet gloves
  hold your eyes

  from wanderlust
  in
  under the clunker

      speech begins
      when hot water
      fills the tub

[5]

Suspect the mind

    when it mothers

    one indefinite
    clue:

        the heart
        harness

        is saccharine

[6]

not about a thing

    under
        adored

        one envelop
        overlaps
        the other

        to the floor

    an audible
    can change the draw

    auspicious

    to a box

[7]

strange lack of affect

     just ear
     of your glossy career

          how agile, gadfly

          gabbing about luck

          no longer
          illegible
to an untrained
     private eye

     I don't get it

          attitude
               is deference
               to
               what

               tympanic
               result?

[8]

artifice

       artsy face
       proper name
       puddin tain
can it be pure
       love?

            walk down
            beside me

            this one's on me,
            my guts

            clown

                just to wash
                you

                my tongue

                at
                that
                thought
                    in
                    that warm cave
                    mother

[9]

Glitter, bird wings

    fly on cymbals

        humble
        arsenic

        cinder room
        light of scent
            pure wind
            wind with everything
            left

        nostrils
        smell
        home

[10]

Grieve the work
    undone, not

      the death drone

      a homiletic
      for an epileptic

         jumps
life is not daisy
    driving crazy sun

up and down

     work real easy
     beach fun
     Sunday

no like

boots in the saddle
   no hirsute rattle
   bones from cattle
   play for some chattel
   calendar battle
     dig a hole
     contest sleep

[11]

obelisks obscure
        the mortal lie, it

    waits, a mask

    gilt
            with perks

    God on your side

                no cause
                because

                stay dark, you one

I want you
            to raise my hand

                palm up
                say nascent sky

[12]

do I immolate
        the rafters
        of passion

to make a rhyme?

Do I harbinge
        the deep bingo
chicanery
of amplitudinous
        beauty?

Do I apple your
        eye glad
        to seize

                me savvy

                vowel
                purr?

Am I too cold, dogweed
        for a dragon
        to languor

        sour spur
        flower next week?

[13]

some words
        are dure
        lapses like a mountain

        strain

old moss
        rathering

        no wound

all words swords
tilted left

no mail
applied

none needed

[14]

a penitentiary
        disease
                is dereliction

        word
        between word

        viper

                let me light a candle

                a soul passes

                in a plane
                heading
                southwest

                like ash

                between your
                teeth

                say him
                Peace

This book was designed by Carl Lehmann-Haupt. It was set in Electra, a typeface designed by the American type designer, W. A. Dwiggins. It was printed, in an edition of 250 copies by BookMobile.